HAL•LEONARD
INSTRUMENTAL
PLAY-ALONG

AUDIO
ACCESS
INCLUDED

TRUMPET

QUEEN
UPDATED EDITION

PLAYBACK+
Speed • Pitch • Balance • Loop

To access audio visit:
www.halleonard.com/mylibrary

"Enter Code"
1249-3065-5308-4769

© Jorgen Angel/CTSIMAGES
Audio arrangements by Peter Deneff

ISBN 978-1-5400-3842-5

HAL•LEONARD®

Visit Hal Leonard Online at
www.halleonard.com

Contact Us:
Hal Leonard
7777 West Bluemound Road
Milwaukee, WI 53213
Email: info@halleonard.com

In Europe contact:
Hal Leonard Europe Limited
42 Wigmore Street
Marylebone, London, W1U 2RN
Email: info@halleonardeurope.com

In Australia contact:
Hal Leonard Australia Pty. Ltd.
4 Lentara Court
Cheltenham, Victoria, 3192 Australia
Email: info@halleonard.com.au

ANOTHER ONE BITES THE DUST

TRUMPET

Words and Music by
JOHN DEACON

CRAZY LITTLE THING CALLED LOVE

TRUMPET

Words and Music by
FREDDIE MERCURY

BICYCLE RACE

TRUMPET

Words and Music by
FREDDIE MERCURY

BOHEMIAN RHAPSODY

TRUMPET

Words and Music by
FREDDIE MERCURY

Hard Rock Shuffle

Slow Rock

FAT BOTTOMED GIRLS

TRUMPET

Words and Music by
BRIAN MAY

I WANT IT ALL

TRUMPET

Words and Music by FREDDIE MERCURY,
BRIAN MAY, ROGER TAYLOR
and JOHN DEACON

DON'T STOP ME NOW

TRUMPET

Words and Music by
FREDDIE MERCURY

I WANT TO BREAK FREE

TRUMPET

Words and Music by
JOHN DEACON

PLAY THE GAME

TRUMPET

Words and Music by
FREDDIE MERCURY

KILLER QUEEN

TRUMPET

Words and Music by
FREDDIE MERCURY

D.S. al Coda

CODA

RADIO GA GA

TRUMPET

Words and Music by
ROGER TAYLOR

SAVE ME

TRUMPET

Words and Music by
BRIAN MAY

(small notes optional)

SOMEBODY TO LOVE

TRUMPET

Words and Music by
FREDDIE MERCURY

UNDER PRESSURE

TRUMPET

Words and Music by FREDDIE MERCURY,
JOHN DEACON, BRIAN MAY,
ROGER TAYLOR and DAVID BOWIE

WE ARE THE CHAMPIONS

Words and Music by
FREDDIE MERCURY

TRUMPET

WE WILL ROCK YOU

TRUMPET

Words and Music by
BRIAN MAY

YOU'RE MY BEST FRIEND

TRUMPET

Words and Music by
JOHN DEACON